AIRPORT LIFE

How to Relate at Any Altitude

JEFF PASQUALE

For more information, visit **www.JeffPasquale.com.**

Editor: Kammy Wood

Text layout and design: Făgăraş Codruţ Sebastian

Cover concept: Maura Pasquale, Vanessa Nicole Ortiz, and

Făgăraş Codruţ Sebastian

For M. and V.

Contents

In an airplane, we're separated from the world while we are simultaneously placed with a hundred or so other people, all of whom are exciting and odd in their own way.

On the whole, life is mostly about interacting with other people—how we get along, or not; how we understand one another, or not; how we support one another, or not. And on a deeper, more subtle level, life consists of the little decisions we make each day and the actions we take to support those decisions. It all adds up to whether we're content and optimistic, or eternally peeved.

Traveling is a process. When we take the subway, planning is required. We have a fallback if we miss our train, because another will be along shortly. When we miss our plane, however, we could be waiting hours or even days for the next one. So patience and planning is necessary with air travel.

The great thing about flying is that once you're airborne, you're suddenly released from the day-to-day challenges we all face. There are no phone calls, interruptions, or delays. Life is temporarily put on hold as we traverse the state, the country, or continents, so we have free time to think.

There are some people who swear that they do their best thinking while airborne. Whether it's the physical or mental separation from the world below or the feeling of flight, it doesn't matter. It's private space and time to reflect inward.

Air travel is an opportunity to view life from 7 miles up—an opportunity to look at your life from a distance, where inconveniences and immediate threats to your time have no impact.

But here's the thing—we don't need to wait until our next airplane trip to give us the time and the space for some serious thinking to happen.

As you read this book (whether in the air or in your bed), consider your life and your circumstances as they are right now. Are you happy? Are you feeling frustrated, cranky, or impatient?

Do you know why?

The minute we walk out the door (or check our bags curbside), we are wearing the face we've chosen. We choose to be helpful or caustic, open or distant, thoughtful or thoughtless. And each one of these choices affects the quality (and the quantity) of our relationships.

It's all about how we relate.

I PLANNING AND PREPARATIONS

T he secret to accomplishing most things we set out to do can be summed up in three verbs: plan, prepare, and execute.

People can spend hours dreaming about what they want, or what they're going to do, but without doing the necessary work, the plan won't come to life.

If you fail to get to the airport on time, or to check your pocket to make sure you have your boarding pass, then you have failed to execute properly, and your trip may not go according to plan.

Whether your trip is for business or pleasure, you must also plan and prepare for the moments when you have to communicate with other people. (The Internet can't do everything.)

You'll need to interact with the cab driver, flight attendant, and possibly the hotel concierge. Will you treat them as people who (genuinely) want to help you have a great trip?

Relating is about courtesy and respect. (It's not about getting people to like you.) Relating is all about getting along with other people—spectacularly.

You may have big plans, and you may have done all of the necessary legwork to allow for amazing things to happen, but it doesn't give you the right to be rude or to ignore people who want to help make your adventure even better.

Wᵉ all wish we could avoid security lines. Or avoid waiting for takeoffs. Layovers. Waiting.

Almost everyone avoids something in their lives. For some, it might be confrontation. For others, it might be commitment.

Consequences vary according to each situation. Wait too long to make an offer on that car in the showroom and it could be picked up by someone else. Date someone for too long without talking marriage, and that person may one day disappear. Hesitate to accept a job offer from the company you've always wanted to work for, and—you get the idea.

Commitment isn't a bad thing. it is a necessary step for any journey. Shyness or resistance to commitments can have an adverse impact on your relationships. Aversion to commitment can come across as an unwillingness to understand the other person. The inability to answer a simple question can leave the other person filling in the blanks, wondering if a relationship is worth the trouble.

Avoidance will almost always come back to bite you.

Plan to commit and commit to a plan. The sooner you purchase that ticket, make an offer on that car, or accept that job offer, the sooner you will embark on the next phase of your journey.

The running joke in many families usually targets the last-minute packer. The last-minute packer traditionally waits until midnight (the day of a big trip) to start packing.

Living last-minute is obviously a recipe for stress, disappointment, impatience, and possibly a bit of anger. If this is you, you're not alone. That's the good news. The other news is that you probably experience stress, frustration, and disappointment on a regular basis.

Organization (and staying organized) is a critical life skill. It isn't about keeping the pens in your drawer all lined up. When you're organized, you gain the time and the space to let other people into your life, and you can actually enjoy your life more.

Far too many people wing it and hope that things will come together in the end.

The odds rarely work out in their favor. They miss a lot of flights.

When you're organized and aligned, life goes a little more smoothly, and you're less likely to find yourself in the security line, scrambling to find your ID and boarding pass.

II | CIRCUMSTANCES AND DECISIONS

```
20 C34B   Delayed
10 C44    Delayed
12 C44B   Delayed
10 C46    Delayed
```

One of the most elusive commodities on the planet is clarity.

Whether it's getting accurate ETA information about your flight from the airline or avoiding ambiguity as you explain to an associate what you need in your monthly report, there never seems to be an ample supply of clarity.

Sometimes it's because we're sloppy, while other times we're just rushed. And unfortunately there are some instances where we're being deceitful. Regardless of our motives, the net results of being vague or unclear are mistrust, accidents, mistakes, or hurt feelings.

We won't always have time to be explicit, though we can and should make the effort in order to avoid a negative outcome.

Clarity is:

"Flight 909 will be approximately 20 minutes late because of weather."

"I enjoy working with you. Would you mind coming by tomorrow to help me again?"

"This drink is too strong; would you dilute it for me?"

"I need three copies of your monthly report on my desk by 5. Is that doable?"

Clarity and truth go hand in hand.

Say what you mean. Mean what you say.

Life will level off for you if you develop and practice the habit of being clear.

G o ahead; just try subjecting a TSA agent to your bad mood.

It won't work.

There's a good chance that when you're going through airport security, you stand up a little straighter, look the agent right in the eye when you're spoken to, and respond with more than a *hmph*.

Why do you act differently with strangers? Because you know you can get away with it.

It's a choice to act badly out of self-importance, revenge, or a lack of self confidence.

(It's true, isn't it?)

A bad mood (and staying in one) is a choice.

Everyone fears losing something. We often fear missing out on opportunities—without realizing it.

Boarding a plane can be similar to a Black Friday crowd waiting outside a big department store moments before the doors open. There are elbows and swaying hips all angling to get into a better position.

Part of the frenzy is attributed to the scarcity mentality that has been forced upon us. Advertisers have gotten particularly good at creating a sense of urgency. In order to sell more of a product, they infer or express that there is a possible shortage. The shortage may be real or it may be a gimmick, but people will respond as if it is real, and that's what retailers count on.

Airlines follow the same line when they overbook flights. This is expressly done to cover themselves and to increase the odds of filling every seat on the plane. We don't always know if the plane is overbooked or not, so we trudge through the line, ready to do battle.

Fear of loss goes way beyond an airport gateway line. Regrettably, modern life has taught many of us that *we must fight for a place in line not necessarily to win, but to avoid losing.*

Sometimes the pull of consumption and possession is just too much. Logic and caring go out the window. And all we can obsess about is getting that *thing*—that seat, that space, or that status.

It's nearly guaranteed that you will never feel settled if you focus too hard on the *chance* of missing out on something.

In the final analysis, it doesn't matter how many times you succeed at capturing a prize; it will never be enough. Its attainment yields only a temporary victory, if you can call it that.

Saving your energy for what's important will do wonders for your life, especially your relationships.

It's easy to imagine confinement in the context of an airplane ride. And it's easy to conjure up all sorts of outlandish scenarios.

Let's go worst case. You are on a three-hour flight, you are in the center seat, and you are exhausted because it's 10 o'clock at night. Now, make things interesting—the person to your right is sneezing incessantly, the people behind you have small children who are making all sorts of noise, and one of them is kicking the back of your seat. Now add some additional discomfort to your situation: you have a pounding headache and you're hungry.

What would you do? What would you say? It is difficult to relate well to others if we're feeling confined.

Confinement usually takes its toll on us because we're not prepared.

We may initially shrug it off as an extremely remote possibility until that moment of truth arrives and we're stuck in the above-mentioned center seat.

Most of us can deal with confinement like this for an hour or two but if the journey goes longer, like a cross-country or trans-Atlantic flight, then confinement is a big deal.

In life it's no different. It is easy to feel confined physically, psychologically, financially—in your job, or even in your own house. None of these issues are game changers in the short term, but in the long run they can have a big impact on your state of mind.

Confinement can mean different things to different people. The feeling may come from a hovering boss, a nosy neighbor, or in-laws that visit three times a week. We tend to overlook the small confinements that creep into our lives without notice, until one day we just let loose.

It's important to know our limits. Attempting to relate effectively when our emotions are high can be futile. Sometimes it's best to wait until strong emotions have passed before seeking to communicate with someone.

Know yourself well enough, and you can avoid confining situations. On a plane, reserve an aisle seat. In life, set and maintain strong boundaries for yourself. With strong boundaries, you can protect yourself and your space by informing transgressors of your boundaries *before* you lose control.

If you haven't noticed before, there are some air travelers who will go through a series of rituals prior to takeoff. They may make the sign of the cross, or bow their head in prayer, or uncross their feet and arms.

Rituals are different from habits because they tend to be more empowering on a mental and spiritual level. Rituals are conscious; habits are automatic. Throwing salt over your shoulder is not a ritual.

Most rituals have meaning. Rituals are intentional acts that almost always help us develop a deeper appreciation for how we live. We rely on them to relieve stress, or to give us a chance to be closer to God.

A habit is simply a routine or a pattern we have developed for a reason, like brushing your teeth or looking both ways before crossing the street.

The challenge we face with our rituals is that it's easy for them to become habits, thereby lessening their intended power. When a ritual becomes a habit, we start performing it without thought.

Rituals can serve us. Whether we're preparing ourselves for the plane's takeoff or we're saying our prayers before bed, a ritual has the power to help us get through stressful times and help us find deeper meaning in the everyday.

Rituals can have a positive halo effect on all of our relationships.

We embrace rituals to add meaning or significance to our lives. They help us find a place to become stronger, calmer, more balanced or enlightened. And the benefits can't help but improve how we relate to others.

III | ATTITUDES AND FEELINGS

We have all witnessed a scene like this before:

An airline gate attendant cannot accommodate a passenger with a change request, or there is an unforeseen delay, and suddenly this peaceful-looking mother of two turns into a screaming, sputtering monster who slings expletives like bags of peanuts at a baseball game.

What happened?

A line was crossed, a button was pushed, or patience was just worn too thin. Everyone's tolerance level is different; but what is the same among all of us is our ability to control ourselves. We all have that power, but sometimes we allow circumstances to prevail, and ... well.

Patience is a lifetime investment for your soul and psyche.

Patience is an important ingredient in relating well with others. Some of us are very good at it, and others perpetually struggle. Even the best of us will struggle with it from time to time. For the long haul, if you flex your patience muscle on a regular basis, you will learn greater empathy.

You may think patience is simply biting your tongue. But impatience can do real damage to your mind, your body, and your relationships. Patience is really the art of giving—giving freely of your time, your talent, and giving others the benefit of the doubt.

Patience is how we respond to trying situations. And almost every trying situation involves people, which means we are responding (and relating) to people as well as the situation.

Patience while traveling means smiling and saying, "No problem," even when you know you're upset. Or you can choose to completely lose it over the length of the flight voucher line, even though you have no control over it.

When you allow impatience to rule, you make the situation all about you and your needs.

Choose to be a good role model. Practice equanimity, be gracious, and give someone the benefit of the doubt. What could it possibly cost you?

At the airport, even if you board your plane and it pulls away from the gate on time, that doesn't mean you'll take off on time, or that you'll land on time, either. Hey, stuff happens. Even life in the fast lane slows down for breakdowns and bad weather. Life interrupted is simply a reminder to be prepared for slowdowns.

Sometimes you may need to change planes mid-trip. It's just an interruption.

If your first instinct upon learning that your flight is delayed is to mouth off or complain, you probably struggle with relating well with others.

Be aware—how you respond to interruptions is nearly always a reflection of who you are and what your level of self-importance is.

When we respond gracefully to an interruption, it's usually because we have thought through some possible scenarios that may unfold, or we have conditioned ourselves not to react with emotion, but to respond from a more neutral or balanced place in our heads, without drama or an adrenaline rush.

There's no need to spend your days crafting ideal responses to all of life's curveballs. It's the big events in life that really require us to relate well with others.

Interruptions and complications are an everyday part of life. You can give them the power to overshadow your plans, or you can gracefully make the best of the situation for you and those around you.

We've all come up against people who, despite our best attempts to be helpful or kind to them, are determined to be arrogant or rude to us. We have choices in these situations, but there could be tension if you find yourself on an airplane sitting next to someone intent on taking his or her bad day out on you. You may need to stand your ground and protect your boundaries.

That person's anger may be directed towards someone or something else, yet the unfortunate reality is that you will have to witness that person's experiment in self-importance. Sometimes suffering fools gladly is the high ground.

But what if you are the culprit? What if you are the angry person? Why are you determined to be angry?

A bad mood or attitude is always your choice.

If you ever notice that you're having trouble relating to other people, consider where your own attitude is currently residing. If it lives somewhere near a place called "Life is Unfair," then you'd best consider relocating your attitude to a better spot. If your belief is that life is unfairly difficult, there is a tremendously high chance that your relationships won't be easy, either.

It is possible to feel your attitude is justified because of some hardship in your life. That's fine, and it's certainly your right.

There is a way to help you determine whether what you're feeling is anger or irritation. If what you're saying (or doing) is hurtful to other people, it's anger; if you're trying to correct a wrong, and it's making others uncomfortable, it's just irritation. Keep going. But remember to be respectful.

As French philosopher André Comte-Sponville wrote, "...politeness is the first virtue, and the origin perhaps of all the others."

If you feel compelled to speak out because you're unhappy or displeased about something that you feel strongly about, be respectful, but be quick. (There is rarely a need to go on about anything for more than twenty minutes, yet we all know people who are masters at it.)

In the long run, remembering to be polite is almost always more important than remembering to be right, be first, or be in control. Politeness will always serve to improve relationships.

Enjoying other people is a big challenge for the majority of us.

This is because we tend to overanalyze other people's words and actions to the point where it's virtually impossible to enjoy their company.

Typically we like people who like us, and this reciprocation is the cornerstone to most of our relationships, whether steady or casual.

This exercise works 90% of the time in the bubble we call our world. But for that remaining 10% of the time, which includes airline travel, we are exposed to total strangers who will do and say almost anything, and there's nothing we can do about it.

Incidentally, the solution to learning to like people outside of your bubble is to turn off or shut down the judge in your head.

You know you do it. We all do it. So the question is: how much do we judge and to what degree does it affect our ability to enjoy (and accept) total strangers?

If it's not universally offensive, does it really matter what she's wearing? Does it really matter what he's saying?

Does it really matter that she chews her gum with her mouth open? Does it really matter that he drives a Prius?

Really?

By the way, I exaggerated the size of our bubbles; it's not 90%, it's more like 20%. So unless you have servants and chauffeurs to do things for you, your bubble is quite small, which means your opportunity to enjoy other people is around the 80% range.

Do yourself a favor and try starting a conversation with a stranger—your seatmate, for example. That's right, a total stranger.

Purposely shift your life by popping that bubble. When you're consistently able to enjoy other people, your level of contentment can only go up.

Some people have the tendency to be exceptionally territorial. And when it comes to seats at an airport terminal, they would erect fences if they could.

All methods of obstruction are employed—bags, books, coats, and food are the usual tools, along with the ever-popular leg over the armrest. It may be more selfishness than a personal aversion to other people. With one glance, though, you will know if you have encroached upon a space hog's terrain.

When you block seats at the airport terminal, you create isolation.

When you isolate, you block yourself from the relating to the outside world.

But a tendency to isolate isn't always an indication of antisocial behavior. Perhaps it's out of fear—fear that stems from insecurity, germ phobia, or social awkwardness. Or maybe it's a lack of desire to deal with others. Sometimes people automatically feel they deserve more space in a public place.

People who hog space also tend to accumulate an overabundance of stuff. After all, they use their stuff to delineate their territory and block outsiders from coming in.

Hoggy ones can be extremely possessive about their stuff, even if it's just a beat up vinyl airport seat.

The next time you decide to spread your stuff across a couple of airport terminal seats, ask yourself—are you a hog? Or are you just inconsiderate?

IV | RESPONDING

Life will almost certainly shake us up from time to time, on a plane or otherwise. Turbulence happens, just like life happens.

Whether you're flying at 35,000 feet and things start shaking, or you're sitting in your living room and unwelcome news arrives, like death, divorce, or bankruptcy, rough patches are part of life.

The way we come through these challenges is *with other people.*

We have the power to heal ourselves. We can withdraw from the world and emerge six months later in better shape. But why wait so long? Strong relating skills can help us immensely when turbulence strikes.

People help people in difficult times. It's a huge blessing.

When turbulence occurs in your life, *relate*. Don't withdraw.

"*Into each life some rain must fall.*"
– Henry Wadsworth Longfellow

Not everyone knows how to ask for assistance.

Do you bark out an order or assume a condescending tone?

Or do you speak in a neutral tone and make an appeal that's from the head and the heart?

There will be times when we can't be polite; we need immediate help. So we can be excused in those cases. But for the remaining 99% of the time, there is no excuse.

It's such a simple thing to do, and yet so many people let their egos get in the way.

They don't want other people to see them as needy or weak, so they make demands:

A flight attendant hears "Hey, I want my drink now!" rather than, "Excuse me, could you please bring me my drink?"

Strangers at an airport hear: "Out of my way!" instead of, "Pardon me, thank you."

In a theater, on a plane—well, anywhere: "You're in my seat," instead of, "I think you're in my seat."

Word choice matters. One or two words in either direction can turn things the wrong way.

The art of relating well means that you speak to others in the same manner you wish to be spoken to.

It's pretty simple.

On a plane trip, it's easy to spot the oddness in others when we're confined and we have time on our hands to be more observant. But what's not so easy is accepting the fact that other people may be looking at us in the same way.

People are odd; no news there. We are all weird and strange in our own way, even if we are not aware of it ourselves.

The odd behavior that you notice on an airplane probably won't harm you or change your life, so consider avoiding the urge to fix or judge it. So what if the person across from you has a really twitchy nose?

Hopefully you've reached an age where you don't really care what other people think about you because you've learned that people will believe what they want regardless of what you do or say.

In simple terms, unless someone's behavior is hurting or threatening you or someone else, it's best to just ignore it. The way we do this is by turning off the critical voice that resides in all of us.

We turn off that judgmental voice through acceptance. Acceptance isn't as much a habit as it is a choice.

We *choose* to accept people and things as they are, or we don't.

We can't change adults, no matter how odd they are.

We can't always change circumstances, but we can change our response to them.

We all occasionally have the urge to control people and things, even when the individuals and situations in question have nothing to do with us. It's in our attempt to control that we usually struggle the most with relating to other people, because we become so fixated on having things our way. When we focus more on being right, we subsequently stop considering what other people think or feel.

People instinctively know when they're being ignored.

Relating to other people won't always easy, but we have to figure out how to do it. If it were easy, there wouldn't be lawsuits, wars, and road rage taking place on a daily basis.

When you're faced with circumstances and people who seem slightly off center, mentally step back and observe. Most of the time it's best just to let it go.

Some people find it amazing that they can sit in a chair at 35,000 feet in the air while traveling 450 miles per hour. Others would rather complain about the weather.

Thankfully, many find amazement in a sunset, or a baby's smile, or in a flower that's just bloomed.

We can be amazed spontaneously, and we can be amazed by choice. Conscious amazement is on the same frequency as curiosity and gratitude; there are elements of surprise and wonder built right in.

When we are amazed, we acknowledge that there is a bigger power at play—

something that allows these things to happen.

If you look into the eyes of your fellow travelers, you will notice just how few people are amazed by anything.

Whether it's our freedoms, our accomplishments, or our health, we have so many things we could be astonished by, if we would only take the time to look. Instead what we see in people's eyes on a daily basis is indifference, unhappiness, and dissatisfaction.

Many people are surprised by people who are consistently surprised by life. They watch and see that they laugh, they sing, and that they are fearless in sharing their amazement with others. They are not dunderheads. (Though some people judge them to be.) People who appreciate surprise have simply moved beyond the fear of judgment to a place that allows them to fully connect.

It's contagious and inspiring to cross paths with people who see the energy and possibilities around them. Non-amazed people who share a space with such positive people often begin their own quest to seek amazement.

So if you happen to be seated next to someone with a life-appreciating grin on his or her face, give that person some space and some slack. Put the judge in your head in his closet and take a look at what life could be like for you.

V | BEING THERE

A typical reaction from an air traveler who's just discovered his luggage has been lost might be anger—which is a normal reaction as long as it lasts about thirty seconds.

Loss is one of those universal circumstances that we all experience. Remembering this is helpful when you're feeling upset after losing something.

Anger won't get your luggage back any faster, and attacking an employee for something he didn't cause is a display to the world that you're a big-mouth bully. What big mouths don't recognize is that most passersby notice a sputtering lunatic, and not the powerful and intimidating person you believe yourself to be.

The best response I've heard from a fellow airline traveler whose luggage had been lost was laughter, followed by the retort: "You guys did me a big favor. I wanted to get some new clothes and now I have a reason to go and get them."

How do *you* respond when other people lose your stuff?

Do you become angry, aggressive, derogatory, or are you able to take the high road and politely accept what has happened?

Loss and blame seem to go hand-in-hand in life. It's really a shame that they are paired so seamlessly.

It rarely serves anyone well in relationships. For example, if you're in the habit of blaming your spouse every time your keys (or other things) go missing ("You must have moved them somewhere"), you're going to be missing more than your keys before too long.

It seems logical that most people are more forgiving of themselves when something is lost than they are if someone else is at fault.

Forgiving is a healing act of kindness; it's hard to do at first if we're not used to it, though with practice we become better.

When you stop making your baggage (and your other possessions) a condition for happiness, you immediately improve your ability to relate with others.

A Plan B can involve both people and circumstances, which means you will always have a variety of options at your disposal if things don't go according to the original plan.

Plan Bs are those little habits we employ as just-in-case steps. For example, we may decide not to pack all of our important items in one suitcase just in case it gets lost. We might take a snack with us in case food is not available on the flight. Or we might bring extra cash with us in case a cash machine is not nearby.

Plan Bs are important. They become your insurance, your contingencies for when things don't go the way you wanted.

When you have a backup plan, you become better at thinking on your feet; you learn to recognize the alternatives as well as the opportunities. You realize, too, that a change in plans can actually be fun.

The key is to become accustomed to creating your own Plan Bs. When you do, you relate better with others. If the worst happens and a plan doesn't come together, the insurance allows you to continue to stay on a good path with the most important people in your life.

While dealing with life's delays, obstacles, and detours, it's easy to forget exactly what your original plan was.

Don't forget where you're going and why you're going there.

We travel to be with people.

We live, laugh, and cry with people.

That's why we travel.

When we have the chance to travel, we see different cultures and different ways of living and communicating. But if we have the chance to observe long enough, it's easy to see that we all want the same things. We all want kindness and connection. And that's why it's important to relate well.

THE END OF THE FLIGHT IS JUST THE BEGINNING

An airline trip is an opportunity like no other. It can take you places you've never been and lets you see the sights you've always dreamed about. And because of that we should naturally pay more attention during our journey. Not in a fearful or self-conscious way, but in a manner that allows us to be more open to who we really are and more accepting of other people. That's how we improve at relating to others.

Relating is a necessary skill in order to feel capable, confident, and successful.

It's not as if you can measure your success by the number of votes you receive for your relating skills. Your measure of success in relating to others is simply how you feel about the experience, and of course, how others feel about it, too.

The problem is, people won't always tell you how they really feel. So make it a habit to review the interactions (both big and small) that you have with others.

The key is paying attention when you communicate with others. Ask lots of questions, be *fully engaged and immersed* in conversations (whether they're with a dear friend or a total stranger), and then be *fully responsive*. That's relating!

What you'll hopefully notice is that little bit of magic that occurs when you relate to someone. Opportunities can arise, relationships can blossom, and sometimes disasters averted—all because you chose to say hello to the stranger sitting next you.

Relating involves risk—the risk of being judged, rejected, or worse, ignored. But life exposes us to those same risks whether we choose to communicate with others or not.

The word *choice* has been used throughout this book purposely. We can live our lives leaning on excuses to get us through the day, or we can choose to be proactive and reach out and relate to others.

With practice, politeness, civility, honesty, and patience become second nature, and we naturally become better at relating and connecting to those around us.

And our lives become better. So much better than we ever thought possible.

"Everything will be okay in the end.
If it's not okay, it's not the end."
— Fernando Sabino

ASSESSMENT
AND
REVIEW

*A*t the end of a journey, it's always good to reflect on what you have experienced. The self-assessment below is provided as a quick review of what you've just read. You may also use it every few months as a scorecard to help you refocus and reassess how well you are relating to others.

PLANNING & PREPARATIONS –

Beginning any new task usually requires a little bit of forethought and planning. How much time do you invest in these steps?

- I plan thoroughly so that I never miss important deadlines or goals.

- I seldom avoid or hesitate with things that require me to take timely action.

- I quickly deal with routine questions and tasks so that they don't come back to bite me.

- I proactively keep myself organized. I'm not compulsive about it, but I am good at it.

- When executing plans, I make a conscious effort to remain courteous and respectful towards those around me.

CIRCUMSTANCES & DECISIONS

— The circumstances we face and the decisions we make reveal who we are as people when we respond to others. How aware are you of your own tendencies?

- I have two daily habits/goals: to always be clear when communicating, and to always be truthful.

- I treat everyone with the same level of respect and courtesy. I don't reserve good behavior only for my superiors.

- I set goals and work hard with the intention of succeeding. I don't direct my energy simply towards *not losing*.

- I take precautions to avoid being trapped in confining situations. (Examples: establishing strong personal boundaries, booking aisle seats, bringing snacks to long meetings, etc.)

- Whether it's checking myself in the mirror before heading off to work or reviewing my presentation notes a few minutes before the presentation starts, I have established personal rituals that serve me and help me to be my best.

ATTITUDES & FEELINGS –

Regardless of what we are facing, we are always in charge of our attitudes and feelings. Take a moment to evaluate yours.

- I practice patience on a daily basis, as much with myself as with others.

- Although I dislike interruptions or delays, I accept them when they occur. I choose the high road versus griping about things.

- While I do not hesitate to speak up if I'm displeased with someone or something, I am always respectful.

- Throughout my day I make the time to consciously enjoy the people I am with.

- I practice thoughtfulness each day by freely sharing what I can – my time, space, information, etc.

RESPONDING – *How we respond to people and how we treat them is essential to relating well. Are you kind* and *considerate to others?*

- Whenever I hit a rough patch in life, I reach out to the people I trust for support.

- I rarely make demands when I need help. I ask for assistance in a friendly, kind manner.

- I do my best to withhold judgment as much as possible, which enables me to communicate better with others.

- I regularly slow down and allow myself to be surprised by people and the parts of life that I might otherwise take for granted.

- I allow people to be themselves by resisting the urge to control things.

How to Relate at Any Altitude

BEING THERE – *Being totally present and continuously aware are both challenging goals in our busy world. How regularly are you able to stay connected to others?*

- Though I can become as angry as the next person, I've learned how to overcome past setbacks quickly so that I can begin focusing on forming solutions to my problems.

- I avoid blaming automatically when things go wrong or missing.

- It's almost instinctive to create a Plan B when I have big projects and events to work on.

- Although I'm not uncomfortable with being alone, I would rather spend my time in the company of other people.

- Even during stressful times, I work hard at relating well to those around me.

ACKNOWLEDGMENTS

This is the second in the series of "Life" books. This series began with a mischievous little book named Subway Life, which evolved from a handful of stories and a bunch of different voices into a compact guide of coaching insights that was much different from the original manuscript. Without the following individuals, this evolution could not have taken place-for Airport Life and Subway Life...

A big *thank you* to the team that has helped me in the creation and production of my last 8 books: my editor, Kammy Wood, and my book designer Fagaras Codrut Sebastian. These are two professionals whom

I will always admire and appreciate for being in my life.

Thanks also go to Monte Lambert, Tom Seamon, Bill Bone, Kelly Fanelli, Jim Sugarman, Steve Q Shannon, Greg Behl, and Matt Peace for their friendship and support.

One more *thank you* to my daughter, Vanessa Nicole Ortiz, for providing me with her great travel photos (risking suspicion as she snapped away in airport terminals along the east coast).

And a last-but-not-least *thank you* to my wife, Maura, for her input, advice, support, and patience during the creation of this book.

> *"I got a problem, can you relate?"*
> – Eric Clapton, Promises

"Each day we meet
Both demons and Buddhas."
– Santoka Taneda

ABOUT THE AUTHOR

Jeff Pasquale is an Executive and Life Coach who works specifically in the areas of life, leadership, and legacy. He has been coaching for 20 years.

He lives in Boynton Beach, Florida.

More information about Jeff can be found at www.JeffPasquale.com

He is the author of: **The Book of Leader**: A Testament to the Art of Leadership, **The Magic Dance**: Do You Lead, Follow, or Get Out of the Way?, **How BIG is Your Target?**: The Powerof Focus in a Cluttered World, **Looking for SUNSHINE**: A Practical Guide for Dealing with Life's Challenges, **Subway Life**: An Underground Guide to Balanced Living, **Get That Promotion**: Manage Up and Get There Faster, and **Get That New Job**: Self-Coaching Steps That Work.

www.ingramcontent.com/pod-product-compliance
Lightning Source LLC
Chambersburg PA
CBHW050532280326
41933CB00011B/1553